C000319837

THE NEW PLANT LIBRARY

WATER PLANTS

THE NEW PLANT LIBRARY

WATER PLANTS

ANDREW MIKOLAJSKI

Consultant: Peter McHoy
Photography by Peter Anderson

AURA

This edition published in 1997 by
Aura Books plc
14-15 Fairway Drive
Greenford
Middlesex UB6 8PW

© Anness Publishing Limited 1997

Produced by Anness Publishing Limited
Hermes House
88-89 Blackfriars Road
London SE1 8HA

All rights reserved. No part of this publication may be reproduced, stored
in a retrieval system, or transmitted in any way or by any means, electronic,
mechanical, photocopying, recording or otherwise, without the prior
written permission of the copyright holder.

ISBN 0 947793 48 8

Publisher Joanna Lorenz
Senior Editor Clare Nicholson
Designer Caroline Reeves

Printed in Hong Kong

3 5 7 9 10 8 6 4 2

Contents

Introduction

*F*rom the still, silent depths of a northern lake to the sparkle of an Italianate fountain, water is the most mysterious and beguiling of the four elements. Bringing water into the garden gives it a new dimension, greatly extending the range of plants you can grow, as well as contributing a special magic of its own. This book illustrates some of the many beautiful plants that thrive in or near water and shows you how to grow them, whether you plan a large, formal pool, a pond that is a haven for wildlife, or merely wish to add the delicate sound of a fountain to a tiny courtyard or patio.

■ RIGHT

A tranquil expanse of water, well planted around the margins and edge, with the huge leaves of *Gunnera manicata* acting as a focal point in the foreground.

Water in the garden

Water gardening is one of the most rewarding branches of horticulture: water plants include some of the most beautiful subjects for the garden, and nearly all are easy to grow. Gardeners who are lucky enough to have inherited a site that already includes natural water in it will be only too aware of the pleasures; those less fortunate have probably, at some point or other, toyed with the idea of creating a water feature.

Water has long been considered an essential component of garden design, particularly in hot climates. In the past, water features were often an indication of status, as at the gardens of the Villa d'Este at Tivoli, east of Rome, or Versailles, near Paris. These sometimes provided the opportunity for wealthy hosts to play practical jokes: many hapless guests found themselves the victims of the *giochi d'acqua* — sitting on an innocuous-looking bench could trigger jets of drenching water.

Persian gardens also contained water, though with more serious symbolic intent, usually laid out in straight rills and channels. The Alhambra in Granada, Spain, the archetypal Moorish garden, has canals and tanks that seem to be there simply to reflect the exquisite architecture. In more recent times, the French Impressionist Claude Monet made one of the most famous and seductive of water gardens at his house in Giverny, outside Paris, which he filled with the water lilies that became the subject of some of his most famous paintings.

Water features in gardens today generally fall into one of two categories: formal or environmental. The formal water feature is geometric in design, often has a fountain, and may contain fish. Plants, if any, are

■ OPPOSITE

A streamside planting in spring: the huge, shining, cabbage-like leaves of *Lysichiton americanus* unfurl while in the background the starry flowers of *Magnolia* x *loebneri* 'Leonard Messel' can also be seen.

■ BELOW

An informal pool, where nature is allowed to have its way, will soon become a haven for wildlife.

incidental. These work extremely well in large gardens, but you can scale down a formal water feature to suit a smaller plot.

The environmental pool, on the other hand, usually roughly oval or kidney-shaped, is there to attract wildlife and the planting may emphasize native species, though all water plants are equally suitable for both types.

For immediate appeal, if you are short of time, or as an easy alternative for a patio garden, try filling a half barrel or a large bucket with water and adding one or two water lilies.

A pool of any kind can be a danger to small children, but parents can still enjoy water in the garden by opting for a small bubble fountain as described in Formal water features.

Formal water features

Given their architectural quality, formal water features are usually best sited near the house, where they can be seen. It is a good design principle to echo some of the house's proportions; for instance, by making the pool the same size or two to three times as big as one of the windows. You can also play interesting tricks: try positioning the pond so that it reflects light on to a garden ornament or a plant with shiny leaves, such as a wall-trained, evergreen magnolia.

In a severely formal pool, keep planting simple, using one or two water lilies (see Plant catalogue). Emphasize the symmetry of the pool by standing pots in pairs on the perimeter, planted for seasonal interest. Tulips would look good in spring, followed by pelargoniums or bright annuals in summer. In winter, topiary specimens of box, bay or holly would look stylish in matching Versailles cases.

Fountains

At the height of summer, nothing is more refreshing in the day or more soothing in the evening than the sound of a fountain. If you have a large plot, delusions of grandeur and the resources needed to go with them, you could opt for a Versailles-like cascade. If you have only a small garden, you can still enjoy the benefits of flowing water by installing a wall fountain, possibly in the form

■ LEFT
An ambitious pool in the garden of a Victorian terraced house. In the boggy area in the foreground, ragged robin (*Lychnis flos-cuculi*) has taken over from the irises to the right; later, the *Gunnera*, just visible through the iris foliage, will dominate. A purple-leaved *Phormium* in an oriental pot makes a stylish focal point.

of a lion's head or a dolphin. Even the smallest patio has room for a water feature. It might be no more than a stone or resin mask that spews water into a tiny basin below. Most garden centres sell ready-made water features of this type, and they are usually straightforward to install.

To make a bubble fountain, sink a small tank, filled with water and fitted with a submersible pump, into the ground. Cover the tank with a metal grid, then some largish pebbles, and you will have an attractive water feature that is no danger to children (see Alternative water features).

■ ABOVE
This Italianate fountain looks stunning against a plain green background of tightly clipped conifer hedging.

The environmental pond

Gardeners these days are increasingly aware of environmental issues, and many feel that a pool is essential for the sake of the ecology of the garden: it greatly enhances the balance of wildlife in the garden as a whole and goes some way towards alleviating the loss of water meadows from the countryside. Environmental ponds always look best if they are of an irregular shape, echoing those in nature, and a shallow margin is

essential if you want to attract birds and small mammals, such as hedgehogs, to drink the water. For the benefit of the latter, make sure that part of the pond has a very gentle slope, and make a 'beach' with stones of varying sizes. This will give a means of exit to any animal unfortunate enough to fall in the water.

Wildlife in the pond

All manner of wildlife is attracted to water without human intervention. You can speed up the process, however, by begging frog or toad spawn from a neighbour's pond (do not take spawn from the wild). Frogs and toads generally prefer large ponds, but smaller ponds will be attractive to newts. These are all invaluable in the garden, since they eat slugs and snails and other garden pests. Even fish may appear spontaneously, the eggs carried on the feet of birds that visit the water to drink or bathe. If you introduce any fish yourself, bear in mind that some types are carnivorous and may eat frog spawn.

■ OPPOSITE
An informal pool in a suburban garden. The excavated soil was used to make the raised bed, which is retained with local stone and log edging.

You can also expect to spot a number of fascinating insects in or around the water. Many a grotesque-looking creature emerges from the pond in early summer and sheds its outer skin to reveal itself as a beautiful dragonfly or damselfly. Less glamorous insects include water spiders, water beetles and water boatmen. Midges and gnats will probably swarm over the water in the early evening, attracting passing birds. There may be some undesirable intruders, however, such as herons, that may steal your fish, but you can always protect the pond with a covering of netting where they are likely to be a problem.

Water plants

There are many plants that thrive in or near water. Most are luxuriant since, unlike other garden plants, they have a constant or fairly constant source of moisture. Bog plants need reliably moist soil, conditions that also suit most marginal plants, though some of these prefer to have their crowns under water. Floating and oxygenating plants actually grow in the water, their leaves either on or just below the surface, while deep-water plants need up to 91cm (3ft) of water above their crowns.

Bog plants and marginals

If you are lucky enough to have a stream running through your garden, or if you just have a piece of marshy ground, there is a wide range of plants that you can grow which like to have their roots in wet soil, but their crowns above the water level. Many bog plants can be grown as border plants. True marginals need to be planted in shallow water with their crowns just below water level.

Some bog plants are invasive, so check that there is adequate room for them to expand before planting.

Among the earliest bog plants to flower are the marsh marigolds (*Caltha*), which are a delight in early spring with their masses of golden-yellow flowers.

Remember too that some bulbs appreciate damp soil: snowflakes (*Leucojum*), snowdrops (*Galanthus*) and some fritillaries all prefer soil that does not dry out. Where space is no problem, a splendid plant for the spring would be either of the

■ LEFT
Like most other hostas, *H.* 'Tall Boy' appreciates soil that does not dry out; with its tall flowering scapes, it makes a striking addition to a bog garden.

Lysichitons (white *L. camtschatcensis* or yellow *L. americanus*), both of which produce showy, arum-like spathes before the leaves emerge. For the best effect, plant them *en masse* where the shiny leaves will pick up reflections from the water.

Even more imposing, but with a later season of interest, is *Gunnera manicata*. Its huge umbrella-like leaves are the largest of any hardy plant, and they reach up to 3m (10ft) across in good conditions.

In a more restricted space, you can create a similar effect with *Rodgersia pinnata* or the ornamental rhubarb (*Rheum palmatum*). The bold, simple leaves of such plants create points of stasis at the height of summer when the rest of the garden is ablaze with riotous colours as the annuals bloom.

Hostas thrive in damp soil, and astilbes, plants with a long season of interest, would be equally at home. Some of the latter have coppery young foliage that is a strong, attractive feature before the plumes of flowers – ranging from pure white through all shades of pink to deep brick-red – put in an appearance. The colour interest continues into autumn, when the flowers develop into rust-brown seed-heads.

Candelabra primulas (including *P. aurantiaca*, *P. bulleyana* and *P. helodoxa*), their flowers carried in tiers, are among the stars of the river bank in late spring and early summer, the flowers often fragrant and dusky hued. Among their showiest companions would be the *Iris ensata* hybrids, with exotic-looking flowers in a wide range of colours. For interest later in the season, plant the

■ ABOVE

A clump of the bog plant *Iris sibirica* in full flower. The floating water soldier *Stratiotes aloides* is in the background.

Kaffir lily (*Schizostylis*), ligularias or *Lobelia cardinalis*.

Many plants like to have their feet in water – *Iris laevigata*, for example, and its many cultivars, including 'Variegata', which is as notable for its silver-striped leaves as for its flowers.

■ BELOW
**A mature specimen of the water lily
'Attraction' in early summer.**

Some grasses grow well in shallow water. For example, *Glyceria maxima* 'Variegata', *Miscanthus sinensis* 'Zebrinus' and Bowles' golden sedge, *Carex elata* 'Aurea' thrive in the wet.

Oxygenating plants

Unless you intend to use chemicals to keep the pond water clear (see Routine maintenance), submerged plants whose growth remains below water level are essential. These plants, which are referred to as oxygenators, absorb excess mineral salts in the water and starve out any algae. Additionally, they give out oxygen and provide hiding places for fish. Some can get out of hand, however, particularly in a small pool, and may need to be controlled (see Routine maintenance). Though few are striking in their own right, several have attractive features. The curled pondweed (*Potamogeton crispus*), for instance, develops bronze tints if grown in full sun. A few oxygenators also produce flowers, held just above the water level. The water crowfoot (*Ranunculus aquatilis*) has buttercup-like white flowers in early summer; even more desirable is the water violet (*Hottonia palustris*), which has spikes of lilac or white flowers.

Surface floating plants

An interesting group of water plants comprises those with leaves that float on the surface of the water while their roots trail below; they reduce light levels (thus inhibiting algal growth) by covering a proportion of the water. Many surface floaters, such as the frog-bit (*Hydrocharis morsus-ranae*), are deciduous, the plants dropping to the bottom of the pool in autumn to overwinter in the mud as dormant buds. The water soldier (*Stratiotes aloides*) behaves in a similar

■ BELOW

A mature pond planted with sophisticated garden hybrids and self-sown native plants.

manner, but its spiky rosettes float up to just below the water surface in spring, where they lurk until flowering time, when they thrust up into the open air. Another curiosity among this group is the water hyacinth (*Eichhornia crassipes*), a tender plant that flowers reliably only during hot summers but that is worth growing nevertheless for the visual interest of its inflated, bladder-like leaf-stalks.

Deep-water plants

This group comprises plants that have their roots in the mud (or in containers) at the bottom of the pool, with their leaves and flowers resting on the surface. Like floaters, they cut down light levels, but you should aim to cover not more than three-quarters of the water surface. Among the deep water plants, the pretty water hawthorn (*Aponogeton distachyos*) will surprise you with how readily it seeds itself, while *Orontium aquaticum* has flowers that look like smouldering cigarettes.

As attractive as either of these, however, are the aristocrats of the group, the water lilies (*Nymphaea*); indeed, they are some of the most beautiful of all garden plants, and

most gardeners who make a water feature do so with a view to growing at least one.

There is, fortunately, a water lily for every size of pool – there are even miniatures, such as yellow 'Helvola' that spreads to a mere 45cm (1½ft) Water lilies come in a range of colours, from white through all shades of pink, to deepest red, and yellow. Some have double flowers, and many are deliciously scented.

Tropical water lilies extend the colour range into orange and blue. Although tropical water lilies are

really only suitable for frost-free gardens, some extravagant gardeners in colder climates like to treat them almost like bedding plants, heating the water in the pond in early spring to encourage quick growth and discarding the plants when they have finished flowering.

Water lilies should be grown in still water and, once they have been planted (see Stocking the pool), are low-maintenance plants that require very little attention, apart from the removal of any rotting leaves in the autumn.

Plant Catalogue

Bog plants and marginals

In this plant catalogue, the water plants are grouped as follows: bog plants and marginals; floating plants; oxygenating plants; and water lilies. For a description of each group, see Water plants.

■ BELOW
ACORUS GRAMINEUS 'VARIEGATUS'

Marginal water plant of garden origin, though the species comes originally from China and Japan. This variegated variety tends to be a little less hardy than the all-green form. Its grasslike tufts of leaves have creamy white margins and help to provide pockets of interest around the pond in winter. It does well in wet soil or covered with up to 10cm (4in) of water. Height 25cm (10in), spread 15cm (6in). Grow in full sun and divide congested clumps in spring.

■ RIGHT

ASTILBE 'ELIZABETH BLOOM'

Bog plant of garden origin. Pale pink
panicles of flowers appear in summer
above bronze, divided leaves. Height and
spread to 91cm (3ft). Grow in partial
shade and divide the clumps in spring or
autumn.

■ LEFT

ASTILBE 'FANAL'

Bog plant of garden origin. Panicles of
crimson flowers are borne in summer
above bronze, divided leaves. Height and
spread to 91cm (3ft). Grow in partial
shade and divide the clumps in spring or
autumn.

■ ABOVE

CALLA PALUSTRIS (BOG ARUM)

Marginal water plant found in N. Europe, Siberia, Canada and
N.E. USA. Large white spathes that surround the insignificant
flowers appear among heart-shaped, shiny green leaves in spring.
Height 25cm (10in), spread 30cm (1ft). Grow in full sun and
propagate by seed in autumn or division in spring.

■ ABOVE

CALTHA PALUSTRIS (KINGCUP; MARSH
MARIGOLD)

Bog or marginal plant from Europe, N. and C. Asia and N.
America. Shiny yellow, buttercup-like flowers appear in spring
above the dark green leaves. Height 15cm (6in), spread 45cm
(1¹/2ft). Grow in full sun and propagate by seed in autumn or
division in spring or autumn. The cultivar *C .p.* 'Flore Pleno' is
more compact and bears its pompon-like double flowers earlier.
Propagate by division only.

■ RIGHT

CAREX ELATA 'AUREA' (SYN.
C. STRICTA 'AUREA')

Marginal water plant of garden origin
grown for its bright golden yellow leaves.
Height to 40cm (16in), spread 60cm
(2ft). Grow in full sun and divide
congested clumps in spring.

■ LEFT

GLYCERIA MAXIMA
'VARIEGATA' (SYN. *G.
AQUATICA* 'VARIEGATA')

Marginal water plant of garden origin.
Its lance-shaped leaves are striped with
cream. Spikes of greenish flowers appear
in summer. Height 75cm (2$^{1}/_{2}$ft), spread
indefinite. Grow in full sun or partial
shade and divide in spring; in a small
pool, restrict its spread by growing
in a container.

■ RIGHT

HOSTA 'HONEYBELLS'

Bog plant of garden origin. The large, broadly oval, glossy green leaves have slightly wavy edges. In mid-to-late summer, slightly fragrant, bell-shaped, pale lilac or near-white flowers are produced. Height 91cm (3ft), spread 60cm (2ft). Grow in partial shade and divide in spring or autumn.

■ RIGHT

HOSTA VENTRICOSA 'VARIEGATA'

Bog plant of garden origin. The oval leaves, heart-shaped at the base with a satin-like sheen, are streaked and margined with creamy white. Bell-shaped, deep purple flowers appear on tall scapes in late summer. Height and spread 91cm (3ft). Grow in partial shade and divide in spring or autumn.

■ OPPOSITE

GUNNERA MANICATA (GIANT RHUBARB)

Bog plant from S. Brazil and Colombia. Its huge, prickly-edged leaves, reaching 3m (10ft) across or more, are carried on 1.5-2.4m (5-8ft) tall prickly stalks. Green or rust-red flower spikes, to 91cm (3ft) high, appear in spring. Grow in full sun. Propagate by seed in autumn or spring. In cold climates cut down the leaves in late autumn before the first frosts and use them to cover the resting crowns.

■ OPPOSITE

HOSTA SIEBOLDIANA
'ELEGANS'

Bog plant of garden origin. The very
large, substantial leaves are deeply
puckered and are intensely glaucous blue-
green. From early to mid-summer the
virtually white flowers appear among the
leaves on upright scapes. Height and
spread 91cm (3ft) or more. Grow in
partial shade and divide either in
spring or autumn.

■ RIGHT

HOSTA 'SUM AND SUBSTANCE'

Bog plant of garden origin. The large,
substantial puckered leaves have pointed
tips and are greenish to bright yellow,
depending on the degree of sun. Height
and spread 91cm (3ft). Grow in partial
shade and divide in spring or autumn.

■ RIGHT

HOUTTUYNIA CORDATA
'FLORE PLENO'

Bog or marginal plant of garden origin.
Double white flowers appear in summer
above metallic green, heart-shaped leaves
that smell of oranges when crushed. Height
30-45cm (1–1^1/2ft), spread indefinite.
Grow in partial shade and divide in spring
or autumn. 'Chameleon' (syn. 'Variegata';
see inset) has single flowers and is grown
for its showy foliage that is marked with
yellow and red.

■ RIGHT

IRIS
SIBIRICA

Bog plant from
C. and E.
Europe, N.E.
Turkey and
Russia. Its blue-
purple flowers,
marked with
white and gold,
appear in late
spring and early
summer. Height
to 1.2m (4ft),
spread
indefinite. Grow
in full sun and
divide
immediately
after flowering.

■ RIGHT
LIGULARIA DENTATA
'DESDEMONA' (SYN. *SENECIO*
CLIVORUM 'DESDEMONA')

Bog plant of garden origin. In mid- to late
summer, the bright orange, daisy-like
flowers appear above the purplish leaves.
Height 1.2m (4ft), spread 60cm (2ft).
Grow in full sun or partial shade
and divide in spring.

■ RIGHT
LOBELIA CARDINALIS
(CARDINAL FLOWER)

Marginal water plant from N. America. Its
rich red-purple leaves are a feature before
the bright red flowers (see above) open in
late summer. Height 91cm (3ft), spread
23cm (9 in). Grow in full sun and
propagate by seed or division in spring.
In cold climates lift plants before the first
frosts and overwinter in a cold frame.

■ LEFT

LYSICHITON AMERICANUS
(SKUNK CABBAGE)

Bog plant from western N. America. The large, shiny yellow spathes that surround the insignificant flowers appear before the cabbage-like, glossy green leaves emerge. Height and spread 91cm (3ft). Grow in full sun and propagate by seed in summer.

■ RIGHT

*METASEQUOIA
GLYPTOSTROBOIDES* (DAWN REDWOOD)

Deciduous conifer from swampy ground in W. China. It forms a conical tree with bluish-green leaves that turn yellow and red in autumn. Height to 15m (50ft) or more. Grow in full sun and propagate by cuttings taken in mid-summer or late autumn or by seed in autumn or spring.

■ LEFT

MYOSOTIS SCORPIOIDES 'MERMAID' (SYN. *M. PALUSTRIS* 'MERMAID'; 'WATER FORGET-ME-NOT')

Marginal water plant of garden origin. The bright blue flowers are carried all summer above the spoon-shaped, hairy leaves. Height 15cm (6in), spread 60cm (2ft). Propagate by seed in spring.

■ BELOW

PELTIPHYLLUM PELTATUM (SYN. *DARMERA PELTATA*; UMBRELLA PLANT)

Bog plant found from N.W. California to S.W. Oregon. White to bright pink flowers appear on tall stems before the umbrella-like leaves emerge from mid- to late spring. Height to 1.2m (4ft), spread 60cm (2ft). Grow in full sun and propagate by seed in spring or autumn or division in spring.

■ RIGHT

POLYGONUM BISTORTA 'SUPERBUM' (SYN.
BISTORTA MAJOR 'SUPERBUM')

Bog plant of garden origin. Throughout summer, clear pink
flowers appear above the mats of leaves. Height to 75cm (2^1/2ft),
spread 60cm (2ft). Grow in full sun and divide in spring
or autumn.

■ LEFT

PONTEDERIA CORDATA (PICKEREL WEED)

Marginal water plant from N. America. In late summer the
purple-blue flowers appear above the heart-shaped, glossy green
leaves. Height to 75cm (2^1/2ft), spread 45cm (1^1/2ft). Grow in
full sun and propagate by seed or division in spring.

■ OPPOSITE

PRIMULA BULLEYANA

Bog plant from S.W. China. The orange flowers appear in early
summer above the dark green leaves. Height 60cm (2ft), spread
30cm (1ft). Grow in sun or shade and propagate by seed when
ripe or by division after flowering.

■ LEFT
PRIMULA VIALII

Bog plant from China. Purple-blue
flowers, produced in conical spikes, open
from scarlet buds in early summer. The
leaves are light green. Height and spread
to 30cm (1ft). Grow in sun or shade and
propagate by seed when ripe or by
division after flowering.

■ OPPOSITE
PRIMULA JAPONICA

Bog plant from Japan. White, pink or
magenta-red flowers appear from late
spring to mid-summer above the bright
green leaves. Height to 60cm (2ft), spread
to 45cm (1^1/2ft). Grow in sun or shade
and propagate by seed when ripe
or by division after flowering.

■ RIGHT
RHEUM PALMATUM

Bog plant from N.W. China. Panicles of
crimson flowers appear in early summer
above handsome, hand-like leaves. Height
and spread to 2m (6ft). Grow in full sun
and divide in spring.

Floating plants

■ ABOVE
EICHHORNIA CRASSIPES (WATER HYACINTH)

Floating water plant from tropical S. America, widely naturalized throughout the tropics and subtropics. It forms stolons (modified stems) below water level and inflated stems that float and carry glossy, rounded leaves. In hot summers spikes of lilac-blue flowers appear. Height 15-23cm (6-9in), spread to 30cm (1ft), more in favourable conditions. Grow in full sun and propagate by detaching plantlets that form on the stolons during summer. In cool climates, overwinter under glass at 10-13ºC (50-55°F).

■ ABOVE
STRATIOTES ALOIDES (WATER SOLDIER)

Floating water plant found from Europe to Siberia. The rosettes of erect, sword-shaped leaves appear on runners. They are usually submerged but rise above the water surface in early summer, when the white flowers are produced. Height and spread 30cm (1ft). Grow in full sun and propagate by removing plantlets from the runners in summer.

Oxygenating plants

■ BELOW
CALLITRICHE VERNA

Submerged oxygenating plant from N. Africa and Europe. The cress-like leaves die back in winter. Spread indefinite. Grow in full sun and divide in spring or summer.

■ ABOVE
RANUNCULUS AQUATILIS (WATER CROWFOOT)

Oxygenating plant from Europe. It has both floating and submerged leaves, the former rounded and lobed, the latter finely dissected. Pure white, buttercup-like flowers appear above the water in spring and summer. Height 2.5cm (1in) when in flower, spread indefinite. Grow in full sun and divide in spring or summer. *Ranunculus aquatilis* is one of the few flowering oxygenators.

■ BELOW
FONTINALIS ANTIPYRETICA (WATER MOSS; WILLOW MOSS)

Submerged aquatic moss from N. America, Eurasia and N. Africa. The long, slender stems carry small, dark green, oval leaves. Spread indefinite. Grow in sun or partial shade and divide in spring. It can also be grown in running water.

■ BELOW
LAGAROSIPHON MAJOR (SYN. *ELODEA CRISPA*)

Submerged oxygenating plant from S. Africa, now also widespread in Europe and New Zealand. The thick, dark green leaves curve back on long stems. Spread indefinite. Grow in full sun and propagate by division in spring or summer.

Water lilies

■ BELOW
NYMPHAEA 'AMABILIS'

Water lily: plant 15-45cm (6in-1^1/$_2$ft) deep. Pink flowers float on the surface in summer. Spreads to 2m (6ft). Grow in full sun and divide in spring.

■ RIGHT AND BELOW
NYMPHAEA 'ATTRACTION'

Moderately vigorous water lily for a
medium-sized pool (planting depth
15–45cm (6–18in). The cup-shaped, red
flowers open to a star shape and rest on
the floating, bronze-tinged leaves. Spread
to 2m (6ft). Grow in full sun and divide
in spring).

■ RIGHT

NYMPHAEA 'GLADSTONEANA'

Vigorous water lily for a large pool:
planting depth 20-91cm (8in-3ft). The
large white flowers float on the surface
in summer. Spread to 3m (10ft). Grow in
full sun and divide in spring.

■ OPPOSITE

NYMPHAEA 'HERMINE' (SYN. *N*. 'HERMIONE')

Moderately vigorous water lily for a medium-sized pool: planting depth 15-45cm (6in-1^1/2ft). The large white flowers have long petals and float on the surface in summer. Spread to 2m (6ft). Grow in full sun and divide in spring.

■ ABOVE

NYMPHAEA MARLIACEA GROUP 'ROSEA'

Moderately vigorous water lily for a medium-sized pool: planting depth 15-45cm (6in-1^1/2ft). In summer the rose-red flowers appear among floating leaves that are flushed purple on emergence. Spread to 2m (6ft). Grow in full sun and divide in spring.

■ LEFT

NYMPHAEA 'SIR GALAHAD'

Vigorous tropical water lily for a large
pool: planting depth 20-91cm (8in-3ft).
The star-shaped, white flowers open at
night and are held well above the large,
waxy leaves. Spread to 3m (10ft). Grow in
full sun and divide in spring. In cold
climates grow under glass in a heated pool.

■ BELOW

NYMPHAEA PYGMAEA
'HELVOLA'

Miniature water lily for a small pool:
planting depth 10-20cm (4-8in).
The semi-double yellow flowers appear
in summer among leaves that are
mottled with purple or brown. Spread to
45cm (1^{1}/2ft). Grow in full sun and
divide in spring.

Making a pond with a liner

The Grower's Guide

Flexible liners

A flexible pond liner gives you a lot of control over the design of your pond. It can be pleated at the corners to fit a rectangle or square-shaped pond, but it is particularly suitable for an informal pond since it can be cut and folded to fit any shape of hole.

If you plan to make a large pond, a flexible liner will be easier to transport to the site of the new pond than a rigid one.

Flexible pond liners are readily available from most large garden and aquatic centres. Alternatively, you can buy one by mail order, which has the advantage of allowing you to specify the exact shape and size required.

Choose a site for the pond where it will be in sun for at least eight hours of the day during summer. Site it well away from overhanging trees, as these could shed their leaves into the water (see Routine maintenance).

Mark out your pool with a hosepipe or thick rope held in place with short stakes. Decide on the size, shape and position of the pool before you start digging, as it will be very difficult to alter it later.

You will need to check the level as you work. Water will always find its own level, and if one side of the pond is higher than the other, bare liner will show when you fill the pond.

When you excavate the pool, slope the sides at an angle of 20–45°. Making a shallow shelf will increase the range of plants you will be able to grow. You can spread the topsoil you remove – the top 15–30cm (6in–1ft) – on other parts of the garden. Soil from lower down (subsoil), which is infertile, should be taken away or used as infill on other garden projects. Another alternative is to use it to make a raised area for a cascade into the pool.

When you dig the hole for a new pond, keep a straight back and try to bend from the knee as you lift the soil, in order to prevent a back injury.

WHAT SIZE OF LINER?

To calculate the size of a liner, first measure the desired maximum length and width of the pool. Then add on twice the depth to each measurement, plus an additional 15cm (6in) all round to allow for an overlap around the edge. The deepest point of the finished pool should be a minimum of 45cm (18in).

USING A FLEXIBLE LINER

1 Mark out the shape of the pond with a length of hosepipe or rope, then remove any turf and start to excavate the pond. A wheelbarrow will help with the redistribution of the topsoil to other parts of the garden.

2 Make a shelf all around the pond (or at one end only) for marginal plants.

3 Check the level as you work. Correct any discrepancies by mounding up the soil on one side. Make sure there are no sharp stones on the base and sides of the pond that might damage the liner, then line the hole with builder's sand.

4 Spread whatever underlay is recommended by the manufacturer of the liner into the hole. Alternatively, you could use an old piece of carpet or some wetted newspaper.

5 Ease the liner into the hole without stretching it unduly. Cover the base with a layer of topsoil about 7.5cm (3in) deep, then fill the pond with water. (The soil will make the water muddy initially, but will soon settle.)

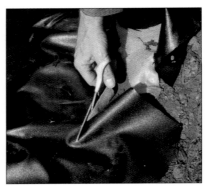

6 Once the pond is full, trim back any excess liner to leave an overlap of about 15cm (6in) all around the edge.

▶

■ BELOW
Once the pond is complete, you can
begin planting (see Stocking the pool).

7 You can cover the overlap with some
of the turf you removed earlier, but
for a neater finish lay paving around the
edge. To disguise the liner, overlap the
water's edge by about 2.5cm (1in).

8 When you are satisfied with the fit,
mortar the paving in position. Be
careful not to drop mortar into the pond,
because this will pollute the water.

PLANTS FOR QUICK RESULTS

Cotula coronopifolia

Elodea canadensis

Houttuynia cordata

Mentha aquatica

Menyanthes trifoliata

Mimulus luteus

Myosotis scorpoides

Myriophyllum verticillatum

Tillaea helmsii (syn T recurva)

Veronica beccabunga

Pre-formed liners

Whatever the advantages of flexible liners, some gardeners prefer to use a rigid pre-formed shell. You know exactly what the finished pond will look like and, before you start work, you can move it around the garden until you find the best position.

Pre-formed liners are usually made of strong plastic or glass-fibre and come in a range of geometric and non-geometric shapes. Most incorporate a marginal shelf or shelves. You will probably also have a choice of colours; black and brown are the most unobtrusive.

Should the liner crack, perhaps as a result of soil subsidence beneath it, empty the pool, remove the liner and repair the damage with a glass-fibre repair kit. Firm the soil carefully before replacing the liner. When the repair is dry, refill the pond.

USING A PRE-FORMED LINER

1 Stand the liner in position and mark the shape of the pool by running a spade around its perimeter and cutting a channel in the ground. A length of hosepipe or rope will define the edge.

2 Begin excavating outside the line you have made. You need to make the hole slightly larger than the liner to allow for easy positioning.

3 Once you have dug to a depth to accommodate any marginal shelves, mark the shape of the deep part of the pond by sitting the liner in the hole and pressing down hard. Dig out the soil about 5cm (2in) deeper than the base of the liner.

4 Put a layer of builder's sand at the bottom of the hole to act as a foundation. Make it deep enough to bring the top of the liner to soil level. Put the liner in the hole. Check that it is level. Backfill with soil at the sides, checking the level as you go. Fill the liner with water, adding a few cm/in of soil at the bottom for any deep-water plants.

Alternative water features

If you do not wish to add a pool to your garden, either because you do not have the space or because you have young children, but you would still like to have a water feature, there are some good alternatives you can consider. These options will enable you to grow some of the plants described in this book.

If you want to grow bog plants but have free-draining soil, all is not lost. It is possible to adapt part of your garden to make a suitable habitat for them. For a natural effect, site the bog garden next to an informal, artificial pool, since the soil surrounding natural pools is usually boggy. The procedure is similar to that outlined in Making a pond with a liner but is less labour intensive, since the lining does not have to be watertight.

Decide on the shape and area of your bog garden and then dig out the soil to a depth of 30-45cm (1-1½ft). Cover the base with builder's sand, followed by a layer of wetted newspaper and then a sheet of lining material of the kind sold for lining ponds. Make drainage holes in the liner with a knife or garden fork, then replace the excavated soil. Water well and then stock with your chosen plants (see Planting a bog plant). You

■ ABOVE
An artificial bog garden planted with *Primula vialii*, *Calla palustris* and other moisture-loving plants. The geranium in the foreground is happiest among the edging stones.

■ ABOVE
A large bucket makes a good 'pond' for this water lily and *Eichhornia crassipes*.

may need to water the bog garden if there are prolonged dry spells during the summer.

You can make a small pool very easily and cheaply by filling a watertight barrel with water. Sink it into the ground first or stand it on the patio as a 'raised' pool. An even cheaper alternative is to use one of the large plastic buckets sold by DIY

■ ABOVE
Ingredients for a bubble fountain: water tank, metal grid, electric pump and cobblestones.

■ ABOVE RIGHT
The finished fountain, here raised slightly above ground level, gives interest to what would otherwise have been a neglected corner of the patio.

stores. You could plant either of these with miniature water lilies or small marginals in pots, stood on bricks at the bottom to raise them to the correct level.

Remember that you will encounter the same problems with a bucket pond as with a large pool, and bear in mind that unless the container is sunk in the ground the water will warm up in summer and cool down in winter faster than in a larger pool.

Such containers are therefore unsuitable for keeping fish, but they can provide good temporary homes for water plants when you empty an existing pool to enlarge it or when you move to a new garden and need to add an instant water feature.

If you have small children, conventional water features pose an unacceptable risk, but you can still enjoy water in the garden by making a bubble fountain. Such a feature perfectly suits a patio and looks attractive even when the power supply is switched off. All you need is a plastic water tank, a wire grid,

cobbles and a submersible water pump (usually supplied with a variety of fittings to produce a spring or single jet of water). Sink the tank in the ground, position the pump, and then fill with water. It is usually recommended that you raise the pump above the tank floor to prevent a build-up of residues in the pump. Then place the mesh on top of the tank and cover with cobbles. Follow the manufacturer's instructions carefully when wiring the pump, or consult a qualified electrician: it is essential that you do not allow water to come into contact with live wires.

Stocking the pool

When deciding what to plant, you need to strike a good balance between bog plants, marginals and deep-water plants; you should also include oxygenators and floating water plants (see Water plants). All stocking is best done in spring when there is less danger of freezing temperatures.

Always buy plants from a reputable source. Most garden centres keep their water plants in tanks of water, and it is worth checking for any signs of blanket weed, duckweed or water snails (for the identification and treatment of these, see Routine maintenance). If the pot the plant is growing in feels at all slimy, reject it. In practice, it is difficult to keep the water entirely free of water snails or pond weeds, particularly if you are given plants by friends from their own ponds, but you do not want to go out of your way to encourage their introduction.

Bog plants can be planted directly into the moist soil surrounding a natural pond, or by a stream, or in an artificial bog garden. You can also grow them in pots stood on the shelves of the pond, but you may need to raise them on bricks to keep the crowns above water level. If growing them in this way, use ordinary pots, plastic or terracotta, not the baskets that are sometimes sold for water plants.

Unless you have a natural stream or very large pond, most marginals and deep-water plants are best grown in containers to restrict their spread. For marginals you can use conventional pots or aquatic planting baskets; deep-water plants are best in baskets. It is often recommended that planting baskets be lined with sacking or a piece of hessian to keep the soil ball intact, but this can cause problems if the lining starts to rot in the pool. To avoid this problem, choose a basket with a fine mesh, so that lining is unnecessary.

Use ordinary garden soil in the containers or compost specially formulated for aquatic plants. The soil should not be too rich, however: excessive nutrients will leach out into the water and encourage algal growth.

Most marginals need about 7.5–15cm (3–6in) of water above their crowns, so you may need to stand pots on bricks to ensure the correct planting depth. When calculating the water depth, measure from the top of the pot.

Young specimens of potentially large, deep-water plants should be planted shallowly to begin with. When planting a young water lily, for instance, make sure that the juvenile leaves float on the surface. As the plant grows and the stems extend, you can gradually lower it until you achieve the final planting depth.

Oxygenating plants and surface floaters do not need to be planted by any conventional method, but simply introduced into the pool.

Planting an oxygenator

To plant an oxygenating water plant, such as the *Lagarosiphon major* shown here, tie it to a stone then drop it in the water. The plant will root in the mud at the bottom of the pool.

Planting *Lagarosiphon major*

Planting a surface floater

Float the plant, here the water hyacinth (*Eichhornia crassipes*), on the surface of the pool. Its roots will trail

Water hyacinth (*Eichhornia crassipes*)

in the water below, allowing the plant to feed on dissolved nutrients. The water hyacinth and other surface floaters therefore succeed best in ponds that have a good balance of plant material that supports a wide range of wildlife. In such a pond, the constant supply of droppings and other waste matter keeps the water high in minerals.

Planting a bog plant

Prior to planting, prepare the site well by forking it over and removing any perennial weeds such as couch grass. Boggy soil naturally retains fertility, so unless you know the soil is poor do not introduce any bulky organic matter such as farmyard manure. This may lead to an excessive build-up of moisture that may damage plant tissue if it freezes in winter.

When planting, take care not to firm in the plants too hard. On wet soil this can result in 'capping' – where the top surface becomes compacted so that air cannot circulate. The soil becomes sour, and lichens and mosses will take hold.

1 Dig a hole large enough to accommodate the plant.

2 Remove the plant from its container and place it in the hole.

3 Firm the plant in gently with your hands then water it well.

Planting a water lily

Water lilies are usually sold both by specialist nurseries that supply by mail order and by garden centres as bare-root plants (i.e. without any soil or compost). They are packed in polythene bags to maintain humidity. For planting a bare-root plant, follow steps 1-3.

Some garden centres, however, occasionally have water lilies for sale as pot-grown plants in large tanks of water. They should be packed in air-tight bags at the point of sale. In both cases, you need to plant the water lilies as quickly as possible to prevent them from drying out.

In ponds where there is a wide range of plant material to attract wildlife, there will be enough nutrients dissolved in the water to make feeding unnecessary. Otherwise, feed with a proprietary aquatic fertilizer applied according to the manufacturer's instructions.

1 Half fill an aquatic planting basket with ordinary garden soil. Place the water lily rhizome on top and continue to fill with soil.

2 Place stones or gravel on the surface to prevent soil from floating out of the basket, and to reduce the risk of fish clouding the water by stirring up mud.

3 (*right*) Flood the basket with water, then gently lower it into the pool to the appropriate depth.

Routine maintenance

Maintaining the water level

You will need to top up the water in the pond periodically, particularly in summer. Allowing the level to drop too much may expose the liner to potentially harmful sun rays. Fill the pond in the evening with a hose. If you can raise the end of the hose above the water level, the resultant agitation will help to oxygenate the water and will be beneficial to any fish in the pond.

Some gardeners like to drain and refill the pond annually, others do it every two or three years. However, it is really only necessary to drain a pond if a leak develops in the liner itself. The tell-tale sign would be a dramatic drop in water level, but before you drain the pond, check the edges to make sure that part of the liner has not collapsed at any point. If any part of the liner has slipped below the desired water level, build it up again from behind, then top up the pool with fresh water. If you are sure there is a leak, press all around the liner with your hands to locate it (the soil behind the hole will feel soft and boggy), then drain the pond to below the level of the leak. Repair the liner, using a repair kit appropriate to the type of liner material.

Keeping the water clear

Most informal pools are self-maintaining, once the balance of plant and insect life is established, and you should have no major problems with water clarity. Algal growth sometimes develops in spring and summer, however, where water lilies and other plants with floating leaves are not mature enough to cover the required area (between 50 and 70 per cent of the water surface). The problem may also be due to an insufficiency of oxygenating plants, but if the pond is a new one, or if you have just replaced all the water, it usually clears of its own accord, given time. Otherwise, check the pool for dead or decaying leaves and flowers, and remove them. To clear the water quickly, use an ultraviolet clarifier.

In a formal pool where the water itself is the prime feature, eliminating algae may require more regular intervention. You can keep the water clear in a variety of ways. If the pool supports no plant or wildlife whatsoever, you can add any proprietary cleaning agent such as the chlorine that is usually added to swimming pools.

If you keep fish in a pool with a few plants, you may need to add an

■ LEFT
When oxygenating plants become congested, lift out clumps with your hands and tear them apart, returning about a half to two-thirds to the water.

ultraviolet clarifier to keep the water clear (see also Ornamental fish). It is easier to keep a large pool clear than a small one.

Pond weeds

Sooner or later, you are almost bound to have problems with blanket weed (*Spirogyra*), a plant that grows beneath the water surface in dense strands and is most prevalent during warm weather. You may not realize you have it until it comes to the surface where it forms unsightly

■ BELOW
This duckweed should be removed before it has a chance to spread. It is very hardy and spreads so quickly that you need to check for it regularly.

masses. It is easy to remove, however, with a long cane, and makes good composting material.

Also in summer you may notice duckweed (*Lemna*), a tiny two-leaved plant with roots that trail in the water. It will rapidly colonize a small pond: once noticed, it should be removed with a net.

Periodically, you may need to thin oxygenators by pulling out clumps with your hands, but make sure that you leave enough behind to ensure water clarity. It is best to thin a little and often.

■ BELOW

To clear water of blanket weed, insert a cane into the water and twist it to wind the weed around it like candyfloss.

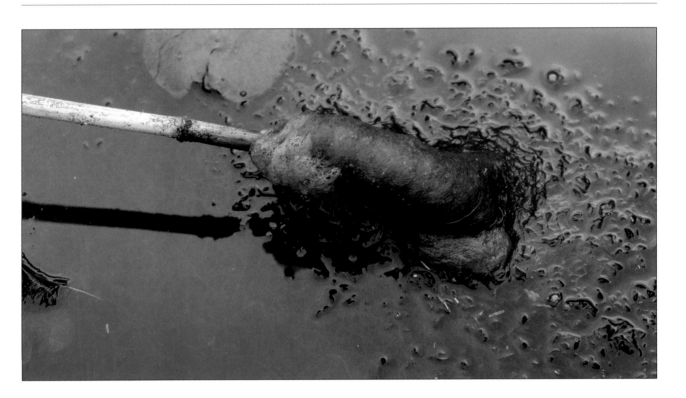

Water snails

Water snails can be a problem, since they feed on plants and often nibble away at the undersides of water lily leaves. You may notice them clinging to the sides of the pool. A few will not do any significant harm and may even help control blanket weed, but you can reduce their numbers by floating a lettuce leaf on the surface of the water and leaving it overnight. Next morning, lift the leaf and dispose of any water snails that have accumulated there. The ramshorn snail (*Planorbis corneus*), however, is a beneficial mollusc, since it feeds on decaying matter at the bottom of the pond.

■ BELOW

If you leave a lettuce leaf on the surface of the water overnight, it will trap water snails that you can then dispose of the following morning.

Propagation

Such is the diversity of water plants that a number of methods of propagation are used. The ones detailed below are those generally practised and are suitable for most of the plants referred to in this book.

Propagation by division

To create new plants that are identical to the parent, you should propagate vegetatively. Division is the simplest method and is suitable for all bog plants that form clumps. It can be used both to increase stock and to thin out congested plants. Dig up the plants in spring or autumn and divide the clumps either by hand or with two garden forks, held back to back. Replant the best pieces and discard any old, woody sections.

Plants that form a rhizome (a thick, modified underground stem) need to be cut into pieces (see Dividing a bog iris), as do water lilies (see Dividing a water lily).

Marginal plants grown in containers rapidly become congested and will need to be divided probably every other year. The iris (*I. pseudacorus*) shown in the step-by-step guide, 'Dividing a bog iris', may also be divided in summer after the plant has flowered.

DIVIDING A BOG IRIS

1 Lift the plant from the pond, and remove any stones from the surface.

3 Open up the plant with your hands to expose the rhizome. Cut through the rhizome with the knife. Make sure each section has a good root system.

2 If the roots have grown through the basket, as here, cut the basket away with a sharp knife. Avoid damaging the roots so far as is possible.

4 Pull the plant apart to free the individual sections.

■ RIGHT
Pot up the sections of the bog iris either individually or in groups, then return the plant to the pond. Spare pieces can be either composted or given to friends.

Propagating by seed

Propagating by seed enables a large stock to be built up quickly for a mass planting, and is the easiest method of raising fast-growing, short-lived plants, such as bog primulas. However, some of the resultant plants will be stronger than others, and not all will necessarily bear flowers of the same colour.

If you want to collect your own seed, allow the seed-heads to develop fully on the plant after flowering.

When they are dry, usually by late summer or early autumn, cut them off the plant and shake the ripe seed onto a piece of clean paper. Either sow the seed immediately or store it in paper bags for sowing the following spring.

Seed is usually available commercially from early spring until autumn, and the temperature required for successful germination is given on the seed packets: some seeds need to be sown in warmth, others need a period of cold.

Annuals sown in spring will flower and complete their life cycle the same year; or sow some in autumn for early flowers the following year. Most perennials grown from seed will flower the second year. For best results, use a proprietary, fine-textured seed compost that is low in nutrients.

Protect summer and autumn sowings in a cold frame over winter; spring sowings can be planted out in a nursery bed when large enough. Keep the developing plants well watered at all times.

PROPAGATING BOG PLANTS BY SEED

1 Fill the base of a seed tray with stones for drainage, then fill the tray with seed compost to within about 1cm (1/2in) of the top.

2 Firm down the compost gently with a tray of the same size. Do not, however, press down so hard as to compact the compost. Moisten the compost by spraying with water. Alternatively, stand the tray in shallow water and allow the top surface of the compost to become damp by capillary action.

3 Scatter the seed thinly and evenly on the surface, then cover with a fine layer of compost. Put the tray in a shaded position and spray regularly to keep the compost moist. When the seedlings are large enough to handle, pot them up and grow them on.

Dividing a water lily

If the leaves of a water lily are raised above the surface of the water, obscuring the flowers, you need to divide it, but it is not practical to split a large plant that is in full growth. For the best results, lift and divide in spring, just as new leaves are beginning to appear on the surface of the water. Unlike other rhizomatous plants, however, you do not need to treat the cut surfaces with fungicide, but can simply replant them. If you wish merely to reduce the size of the plant, cut the rhizome in half, following steps 1–3 on this page, then pot up the pieces into aquatic baskets and return them to the pool as for a new plant (see Stocking the pool). If your aim is to produce many new plants, cut small sections and grow them on in a wet environment, but outside the pool, for about a year before finally planting out.

DIVIDING A WATER LILY

1 Lift the water lily in spring, put it in a bowl of water and wash it free of all soil. Trim back any over-long roots with secateurs and remove any damaged leaves.

2 Cut the rhizome into pieces, making sure each section has roots and leaves or leaf buds.

3 Pot the sections up into pots containing ordinary garden soil, and finish off with gravel to reduce the risk of the soil being disturbed.

4 Put the water lily section in a bowl of water and keep it in a shaded place. New leaves will appear within a few months. After about a year, the plant should be big enough to return to the pool.

Ornamental fish

Ornamental fish are among the least troublesome of pets, and in a formal pond they will delight with their rapid, darting movements. This section describes fish that you can reasonably expect to survive outdoors in climates where frosts are likely in winter. The number of fish you can keep depends on the size of the pool.

When buying fish, check the final size to which they will grow. You need to allow about 0.1sq m (1sq ft) of water per 7.5cm (3in) of fish, depending on the type of fish: double this allowance for very active fish, such as golden orfe, or demanding ones like koi. The pond should have some shaded areas, so that it does not overheat in summer, and also be deep enough, around 60cm (2ft), not to freeze solid in winter, though large fish such as koi may benefit from deeper water.

There should be plenty of oxygenating plants, both to maintain a good balance between oxygen and carbon dioxide, and to provide shelter for any young that may be produced. If you have a fountain, turning it on during the evening, when the plants stop photosynthesizing, will help to oxygenate the water.

If the fish are to be the dominant feature of the pool, and any plants are incidental, you should also add a biological filter for the benefit of the fish. If a small pool is to support a large fish population, this is essential. Biological filters keep the water pure but do not keep it clear. To maintain water clarity in such a situation, use an ultraviolet water clarifier.

Check with the retailer that the fish are hardy enough to survive winters in your area. As well as the fish featured here, golden orfe, golden rudd and golden tench are good pond fish. If it is your intention to keep more than one variety, check with your supplier that they are compatible.

At the point of sale, the fish are usually put into polythene bags with a small amount of water. If you have a long distance to travel, make sure the bag is inflated with oxygen. To introduce them into the pond, place the bag in the water at the edge of the pond. Wait until the temperature of the water in the bag is the same as the pond (usually after about half an hour), then open it and let the fish swim away.

Fish should only be fed while they are active, usually from spring to early autumn. Never give more food than the fish will eat within about 10 minutes: any food left floating on the surface will sink to the bottom of the pool, where it will rot.

In winter, to prevent the whole surface of the water from freezing during cold snaps, use a pond heater to keep a small area ice-free.

Most ornamental fish are likely to be attractive to certain predators, particularly herons. If there is a heron in the vicinity, cover the pool with a net whenever you are absent. Plastic decoy herons are available, but these are seldom effective deterrents and may even attract other herons.

Goldfish

The most popular of ornamental fish, usually solid red-gold in colour with shiny scales, goldfish are suitable for a small pond: adult size is around 15cm (6in). They keep near the surface of the water when active and are reasonably hardy. There are many varieties; some with longer fins and

■ BELOW
Goldfish are among the least demanding and most colourful of pets.

tails, others with white or silver markings. Black goldfish, known as moors, are also available.

Shubunkins

A variety of goldfish but larger, around 20cm (8in), shubunkins have transparent, non-reflective scales that make them appear scale-less. Most combine two or more colours. They have very quick movements and are very hardy.

Comets

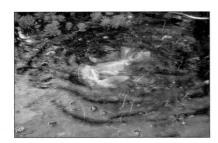

Also a variety of goldfish, comets have longer fins and more streamlined bodies up to 25cm (10in) in length.

■ BELOW
Goldfish are among the least demanding and most colourful of pets.

They are usually red-orange in colour, though other colours are also available. They have rapid movements (occasionally leaping out of the water at breeding time), and are hardy.

Koi

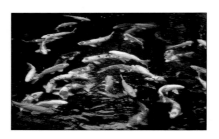

Koi are among the most sought-after (and expensive) of ornamental fish. They mature to 60–91cm (2–3ft) in length. Koi come in a wide variety of colours, including silver, cream, red, blue, gold and black, and are often attractively marked with secondary colours.

Koi tend to disturb the mud on the pond floor, thus clouding the water, so cover the base of a pool that will contain Koi with stones or gravel. They are demanding fish, needing very high water quality and plenty of space, and are for experienced fish-keepers only.

Calendar

Spring

Ponds Make new ponds and plant new stock. Clean out any rubbish or dead plant material that has accumulated in the pond over the winter. Divide marginal plants and water lilies. Start feeding fish that are becoming active after hibernation, and introduce new fish. If you stored the electric pump for a fountain in a dry place during the winter, re-install it in the pond.

Bog gardens Make new artificial bog gardens. Plant new stock and divide congested plants. Sow seed of perennials.

Summer

Ponds Top up artificial ponds regularly, in the evenings. Remove pond weeds. Control algae by adding oxygenators, removing dead plant material, or using an ultraviolet clarifier. Remove water snails that damage plants. Thin congested oxygenating plants.

Bog gardens Gather seed from plants as it ripens. Divide water irises after they have flowered.

Autumn

Ponds Divide marginals. Remove fallen leaves from ponds. Stop feeding ornamental fish as they become less active. Where practical, remove electric pumps from fountains, clean them thoroughly, check the wiring and store in a dry place until the following spring.

Bog gardens Plant new stock. Divide congested plants. Sow seed of perennials and overwinter them in a cold frame.

Winter

Ponds If a pond that supports fish freezes over, melt holes by standing a saucepan of hot water on the ice.

Other recommended water plants

Apart from the plants described and illustrated in the Plant Catalogue, the following are recommended.

Alisma plantago-aquatica (Water plantain) Marginal water plant from Europe, E. Asia, Africa and the USA with pale pink flowers in summer. Height 75cm (2¹/2ft), spread 45cm (1¹/2ft).

Aponogeton distachyos (Water hawthorn) Deep-water plant from S. Africa that produces curious, hawthorn-scented flowers during summer. Spread to 1.2m (4ft).

Aruncus dioicus (syn. *A. sylvester;* Goat's beard) Bog plant from Europe and the Caucasus with panicles of frothy, creamy white flowers in summer. Height 2m

Aruncus dioicus

(6ft), spread 1.2m (4ft).

Azolla caroliniana (Mosquito fern, Fairy moss) Floating water plant from Europe, the USA and the Caribbean with oval, green, pink or bronze-red leaves. Spread indefinite.

Butomus umbellatus (Flowering rush) Marginal water plant from Eurasia with rose-pink flowers in summer. Height 91cm (3ft), spread 45cm (1¹/2ft).

Cardamine pratensis (Cuckoo flower, Lady's smock) Bog plant from Europe with white or lilac flowers, the white ones veined and flushed lilac in spring. Height 30-45 cm (1-1¹/2ft), spread 30cm (1ft). Cultivars include 'Flore Pleno'.

Cotula coronopifolia (Brass buttons) Marginal water plant from S. Africa Produces button-like yellow flowers in summer. Height 15cm (6in), spread 30cm (1ft).

Eriophorum angustifolium (Common cotton grass) Marginal water plant from N. Europe, N. America and the Arctic, with grass-like leaves and cotton-wool-like seed-heads in late summer. Height and

Eriophorum angustifolium

spread 30-45cm (1-1¹/2ft).

Eupatorium purpureum (Joe Pye weed) Bog plant from eastern USA with panicles of pale pink or rose-purple flowers in late summer. Height to 2.1m (7ft), spread to 91cm (3ft).

Filipendula ulmaria 'Aurea' (syn. *Spiraea ulmaria* 'Aurea'; Meadowsweet) Bog plant of garden origin with bright yellow-green leaves. Height and spread 40cm (16in). It is best to remove the flowers.

Geum rivale (Water avens) Bog plant from Europe with bell-shaped, cream, pink or orange flowers. Height and spread 30-45cm (1-1¹/2ft). Cultivars include 'Album' (white) and 'Lionel Cox' (apricot-yellow).

Hemerocallis (Daylily) Genus of bog plants from the Far East. Produces funnel-shaped flowers in a wide range of colours, and grass-like foliage. Height and spread to 91cm (3ft). There are many cultivars, including 'Golden Chimes'

(yellow), 'Marion Vaughn' (pale lemon-yellow), 'Pink Damask' (pink) and 'Stafford'(bright red).

Hemerocallis 'Pink Damask'

Hottonia palustris (Water violet) Oxygenating plant from Europe and W. Asia with whorled leaves and stalks bearing pale lavender flowers that emerge from the water in early summer. Spread indefinite.

Hydrocharis morsus-ranae (Frogbit) Floating water plant from Europe and W. Asia with small, white flowers in summer and miniature water lily-like leaves. Spread to 91cm (3ft) or more.

Hypericum elodes Marginal water plant from W. Europe with bright

yellow flowers in summer. Height to 30cm (1ft), spread 45cm (1¹/2ft).

Iris ensata (syn. *I. kaempferi*, Japanese water iris) Bog plant from Japan, China and Russia. Purple flowers marked with yellow from early to mid-summer. Height to 91cm (3ft), spread indefinite. There are many cultivars, including 'Alba' (white) and 'The Great Mogul' (blackish-purple).

Iris ensata 'The Great Mogul'

Iris laevigata Marginal water plant from E. Asia. Blue or white flowers early to mid-summer. Height to 91cm (3ft), spread in-definite. Cultivars include

'Alba' (white), 'Rose Queen' (rich purple-pink) and 'Variegata' (with cream-striped foliage).

Iris versicolor (Blue flag) Marginal water plant from the USA with blue or purple-blue flowers marked with greenish-yellow. Height 60cm (2ft), spread indefinite. 'Kermesina' has claret-red flowers.

Juncus effusus 'Spiralis' (Corkscrew rush) Marginal water plant of garden origin with slim, cylindrical, contorted leaves. Height 91cm (3ft), spread 60cm (2ft).

Lychnis flos-cuculi (Ragged robin) Bog plant from Europe with pale purple flowers that have deeply segmented petals. Height and spread to 60cm (2ft).

Lythrum salicaria (Purple loosestrife) Bog plant common in Europe and Asia. Naturalized in the USA. Pink-purple flowers from mid-to late summer. Height 60cm-1.5m (2-5ft), spread 45 cm (1½ ft).

Lythrum salicaria

Matteuccia struthiopteris (Ostrich fern, Shuttlecock fern) Fern from damp areas of Europe, E. Asia and N. America with feathery green fronds. Height 91cm (3ft), spread 45cm (1½ft).

Mentha aquatica (Watermint) Marginal water plant from Eurasia with mint-scented leaves and deep lilac flowers. Height 15-91cm (6in-3ft), spread indefinite.

Menyanthes trifoliata (Bog bean, Marsh trefoil) Marginal water plant, widely distributed in the northern hemisphere, with star-shaped white flowers that open from

pink buds in late spring. Height 23cm (9in), spread 30cm (1ft).

Mimulus luteus (Monkey musk, Yellow monkey flower) Bog plant from Chile, naturalized elsewhere, with yellow flowers spotted with dark

Matteuccia struthiopteris

red or purple. Height and spread 30cm (1ft).

Mimulus ringens (Allegheny monkey flower) Marginal water plant from N. America. Violet-blue, pink or white flowers. Height to 60cm (2ft), spread to 23cm (9in).

Myriophyllum verticillatum (Myriad leaf). Oxygenating plant

from N. America, Europe and Asia with whorled leaves, some of which appear above the water surface. Spread indefinite.

Nuphar lutea (Brandy bottle, Yellow water lily) Deep-water plant from the USA, N. Africa and Eurasia with bright yellow flowers and floating leaves. Spread 1.5m (5ft).

Nymphaea 'Escarboucle' Large waterlily with cup-shaped, deep crimson flowers. Spread to 3m (10ft).

Nymphaea 'Firecrest' Small water lily with star-shaped, deep pink flowers. Spread to 1.2m (4ft).

Nymphaea 'Madame Wilfon Gonnère' Medium-sized water lily. Fully double pink flowers age to white. Spread to 1.5m (5ft).

Nymphaea Marliacea Group 'Albida' Medium-sized water lily with scented white flowers. Spread to 2m (6ft).

Orontium aquaticum (Golden club) Deep-water plant from the USA with curious, cylindrical, bright yellow flowers on the ends of white stalks. Spread 60cm (2ft).

Osmunda regalis (Royal fern) Fern from American continent with bright green fronds and (on mature plants) brownish flower spikes. Height 2m (6ft), spread 91cm (3ft).

Peltandra saggitifolia (White arrow arum) Marginal water plant from the USA with white arum-like spathes that surround the yellow flowers that are followed by red berries. Height to 60cm (2ft), spread 30cm (1ft).

Potamogeton crispus (Curled pondweed) Oxygenating plant from Europe, naturalized in the USA, with wavy-edged, seaweed-like leaves. Spread indefinite.

Rodgersia pinnata Bog plant from China with long panicles of red flowers that are carried above striking, hand-like, divided leaves.

Height to 1.2m (4ft), spread 75cm (2½ft). Cultivars include 'Alba' (white flowers), 'Rubra' (deep red) and 'Superba' (bronze-tinted leaves).

Sagittaria sagittifolia Marginal water plant from Eurasia with arrow-shaped leaves and clusters of white flowers. Height 45cm (1½ft), spread 30cm (1ft).

Sagittaria sagittifolia

Saururus cernuus (Swamp lily) Marginal water plant from N. America with drooping spikes of cream flowers. Height 23cm (9in), spread 30cm (1ft).

Schizostylis coccinea (Kaffir lily) Bog plant from S. Africa with spikes of

saucer-shaped, single flowers in autumn to early winter. Height to 60cm (2ft), spread 30cm (1ft). Cultivars include 'Major' (scarlet), 'November Cheer' (deep pink) and 'Viscountess Byng' (clear pink).

Scirpus lacustris subsp. **tabernaemontani 'Zebrinus'** Marginal water plant of garden origin with quill-like leaves, banded with green and white. Height 1.5m (5ft), spread indefinite.

Trapa natans (Water chestnut) Floating water plant from C. Europe, W. Asia and Africa with swollen stems that carry shiny, triangular leaves with serrated edges. Spread 23cm (9in).

Trollius x **cultorum** (Globe flower). Bog plant of garden origin with rounded flowers in late spring. Height to 60cm (2ft), spread 30cm (1ft). Cultivars include 'Alabaster' (white), 'Earliest of All' (bright yellow) and 'Orange Princess'.

Utricularia vulgaris (Greater bladderwort) Floating water plant from Europe, N. Africa and parts of Asia with submerged leaves that bear 'bladders' and yellow flowers in late summer. Spread 30cm (1ft).

Veronica beccabunga (Brooklime) Marginal water plant from Eurasia, naturalized in N. America, with bright blue flowers all summer. Height and spread to 23cm (9in).

Trapa natans

Zantedeschia aethiopica 'Crowborough' (Arum lily) Marginal water plant, with arrow-shaped leaves and showy white spathes surrounding yellow flowers. Height to 91cm (3ft), spread 60cm (2ft).

Index

ACKNOWLEDGEMENTS
The author and publishers would like to thank the following for allowing photography in their gardens: Coton Manor Garden, Coton, Northants; Cottesbrooke Hall Gardens, Northants; Ann Hartley, Long Buckby, Northants; Janine Hurry, Long Buckby, Northants; Mr and Mrs A . Keech, Long Buckby, Northants; Christopher Lloyd, Great Dixter, East Sussex; Peter Oliver, Bath, Avon; The Plantsman, West Haddon, Northants; Stapeley Water Gardens, Nantwich, Cheshire. The pictures on pages 43, 44a, 45b, 58-9 and 60-63 were lent by Peter McHoy.